A Chance to Serve

Books by Chuck Morse

Thunder Out of Boston

(The satirically entitled) *Why I'm a Right Wing Extremist*

*The Difference Between Us and Them-America Confronts
The Leftist-Islamist Axis of Evil*

The Gramsci Factor-59 Socialists in Congress

*The Nazi Connection to Islamic Terrorism—Hitler and Haj Amin al-
Husseini*

A Chance to Serve

✦

A Republican runs for Congress in Massachusetts

First Edition

Chuck Morse

iUniverse, Inc.
New York Lincoln Shanghai

A Chance to Serve
A Republican runs for Congress in Massachusetts

iUniverse, Inc.

For information address:
iUniverse, Inc.
2021 Pine Lake Road, Suite 100
Lincoln, NE 68512
www.iuniverse.com

ISBN: 0-595-30766-3

Printed in the United States of America

This book is dedicated to the people of the Fourth Congressional District who seek a better and more secure future for themselves and their children

Contents

Why I Am Running for Congress

My name is Chuck Morse, I am 47 years old, and I am running for Congress because I want the people of this district to have a real choice in November 2004. One of the reasons for voter apathy has been the lack of meaningful choice in candidates. But this time, you, the voter, when you enter the voting booth, will have a genuine choice, one that is clear and dramatic.

I am a conservative Republican. My opponent is an ultra-liberal Democrat.

As a family man, I am a strong advocate and defender of family values. My opponent represents the aspirations of the cultural elite as a supporter of such causes as gay marriage, partial birth abortion, appeasement, and government by judicial decree.

As a small businessman, I believe in the American free enterprise system, which has made us the richest country in the world. My opponent, as a member of the Progressive Caucus, believes in more onerous regulation of business and more taxes. He has earned a very low rating from the National Taxpayers Union.

All my life I have had to earn a living on the basis of my own efforts and thus oppose oppressive taxation. My opponent has lived off the taxpayer since before he left college and, naturally, he opposed the Bush tax cuts. When he leaves Congress, he will have a retirement pension second to none in the nation.

In other words, in November 2004 you will have two candidates to choose from with two opposing philosophies of life.

Which candidate do you think will serve you better in the Congress of the United States? It's your choice to make.

The Advantage of Having a Republican Representing You in Congress

As a Republican, I will have a welcome access to President Bush's administration. I will be able to convey to the President and his staff the concerns of our constituency. This is important when seeking funding for important projects in our district such as the Boston-New Bedford-Fall River commuter rail line.

It should be noted that President Bush's White House Chief of Staff is Andrew Card, a native of Massachusetts. So there should be no doubt that the needs of the Fourth Congressional District will get the Administration's attention.

That in itself should be a good reason why the voters of the Fourth Congressional District should send a Republican to Washington. They need someone who will be welcomed as a friend of the Republican Administration.

What I Will Bring to the Job of Congressman

For years, as a radio talk-show host, commentator and columnist I have studied how our political system works. I have interviewed hundreds of experts and news-makers on my show, including my opponent, and thus have had to deal with the many national and international crises our nation has faced during the last six years. No university could have given me a better education than the one I got as a talk-show host.

I have interviewed such luminaries of the left as Noam Chomsky, Howard Zinn, Gloria Steinam, and others. Thus, I have a very good idea of what's in their heads, and I know why I could never be one of them.

As a columnist, I have had to do hard research on controversial issues. The result is a solid body of writing about all of the problems that confront America today. My views and beliefs are there for the public to see. I have authored five books, which any voter can read. In other words, I am an open book, and you can read my philosophy of life for yourself.

My opponent is a very partisan politician with very bad judgment. His philosophy of life has been expressed in hundreds of articles, interviews, and speeches. So we know where he stands on just about every issue. What should interest the voters of this district is Barney Frank's voting record in Congress, and it is a very revealing one indeed.

Amber Alert

Did you know that Barney Frank was one of only 25 members of the House of Representatives who voted *against* the Amber Alert bill? The Senate voted for the bill unanimously. Four hundred representatives voted for the bill, including every member of the Massachusetts delegation, except Barney. In fact, it was Barney's vote against Amber Alert that convinced me that I ought to run against him in 2004.

Why was this bill so overwhelmingly supported by Congress? Because it expanded and strengthened the protection of our children from kidnappers. It permits law-enforcement agencies and local broadcasters to send an emergency alert to the public when a child has been abducted. By getting the alert out early enough, the kidnapper may not be able to carry out his plan before being caught.

Named after Amber Hagerman, a 9-year-old Texas schoolgirl who was kidnapped while riding her bicycle and murdered in 1996, the bill was introduced in the Senate by Senator Dianne Feinstein, Democrat from California. According to her office, since 1996 Amber Alert has been credited with the safe return of 43 children to their families, including a case in which a kidnapper released a child after hearing the alert on the radio.

But Barney Frank voted against this bill. Why? He says he voted against it because of the Republican add-ons. What were the add-ons? They were tough measures to punish criminals, pedophiles, and child pornographers. And it was those tough measures that Frank opposed.

President Bush signed Amber Alert into law on April 30, 2003. Present at the signing were Elizabeth Smart, who had been rescued from a kidnapper, and the families of other kidnapped children. Apparently, Barney is much more concerned about the rights of pedophiles and child pornographers than the rights of families in his district who are concerned about child abductions.

As a father of a five-year-old daughter, I would have voted enthusiastically for Amber Alert had I been your representative in Congress.

My Opponent's Ultra-Liberal Votes

Barney Frank's vote on Amber Alert is not the only one where he has shown disinterest in the real interests of his constituents. He has voted consistently as an ultra-liberal:

He voted against **School Vouchers** that would have saved many minority children from educational failure.

He voted against the banning of **Partial Birth Abortions**, one of the most barbaric and cruel medical procedures ever devised.

He voted against the **Defense of Marriage Act**, which the vast majority of Americans favor.

He voted against a bill that would give the government the right to use secret evidence to deport immigrants accused of being terrorists.

He has voted in favor of a federal **hate crimes** bill that would make a crime against a member of a government-selected group more serious than a crime against anyone else.

He has voted for greater restrictions against our **Second Amendment** right to own firearms.

Barney Frank has one of the highest pro-ACLU voting records in Congress.

Two Biographies, Two Lifestyles

My opponent, Barney Frank, has truly lived a charmed life. He went to Harvard, during which time he also worked as an aide to a member of the Massachusetts legislature. Thoroughly steeped in Democratic politics, on graduation from Harvard, he worked for Mayor Kevin White of Boston and then ran for the State Legislature where he stayed for eight years. In 1980, when liberal Father Drinan had to leave Congress as 4th District Representative on orders from the Pope, Frank moved into the district and ran against Republican Margaret Heckler for Drinan's seat. He won and has been there for twelve terms. He owns and lives in a condominium in Washington, D.C. He used the 4th district merely as a stepping-stone for his career.

I, Chuck Morse, on graduating from Quincy High School, went out into the world and got a job. I've been a waiter, a cab driver, and in 1986, I started my own business in advertising distribution. In 1988 I met my future wife Barbara Billig of Merrick, New York, whom I married in 1990. Barbara is an attorney and works for the Federal government. We bought a condominium in Brookline, and now have a five-year-old daughter. We belong to the Kehillath Israel congregation in Brookline and take our religion seriously. In other words, we have planted our roots in the 4th district.

The success of my business permitted me to indulge myself in what I enjoy most: being a radio talk-show host. In that field I have managed to gain a national audience and a reputation as a very sharp interviewer. My years on radio have given me the equivalent of a university education. I've always had an interest in politics, social philosophies, and world events, and my talk shows gave me the opportunity to grow in knowledge and understanding.

In many respects, my family values are very much the same as those of the people in the 4th district whom I wish to represent. I am concerned about taxes and the state of the economy. I am concerned about the education of our children. I am concerned about national security and the war on terrorism. In other words, I am in a much better position and frame of mind to represent your interests and values than is my opponent.

Why I Decided to Run

In May of 2003, a Republican activist in New Bedford, familiar with my views, urged me to run for Congress against Barney Frank. He convinced me that I could win. He made the case that Frank's support is broad but shallow. In the last election, Frank ran unopposed and over 40% of the voters left the ballot blank. As a liberal, Frank is a national figure, but his politics are largely viewed as ineffective in a district that is looking for real influence in Washington.

Up until then I had no political ambitions whatsoever. The thought of running for public office had never occurred to me. On radio, I urged some of my passionate listeners to get involved in politics and run for office. Certainly, in Massachusetts, we need more young Republicans running for the legislature. And now, here was I, tossing my own hat into the ring. But could I win? I took heart from Mitt Romney's victory.

Romney, a Republican businessman, had been elected Governor of this liberal state with a handsome majority against liberal Democrat Shannon O'Brien, state treasurer. Romney almost carried the Fourth Congressional District, which had been viewed, until then, as a "safe" district for the Democrats.

The 4th district is a peculiar mix of upscale liberal Boston suburbs like Brookline and Newton and working class towns like New Bedford and Fall River. The district includes the affluent folk of Dover and the young new homeowners in the many smaller towns. It is a district abounding in small businesses. Family life is still the social mainstay of the district.

Even though the Democrats brought Bill Clinton and Ted Kennedy to campaign for Shannon O'Brien, Romney carried 65% of the cities and towns in the district and lost by a mere fraction of the vote. This indicates that there is a solid base in the district for a Republican candidate.

I Endorse the Romney Platform

Mitt Romney ran on a platform that I proudly and unequivocally endorse. He is holding the line on taxes in a state that is top heavy with an oversized government. Frank, in contrast, voted against President Bush's tax cuts, which have already stimulated the economy and given us economic growth of over 8% in the third quarter of 2003. An astonishing comeback!

Frank has a quarter-century record as a liberal tax and spender. Romney is consolidating and streamlining a patronage-laden state government, while Frank is known as an advocate of bigger government. Romney is taking on the corrupt Beacon Hill political culture, while Frank is part of the problem.

The state election included a libertarian ballot initiative to completely get rid of the state income tax. It received an astonishing 47.5% of the vote, a clear indication that the people of Massachusetts want less taxes, not more as advocated by Democrats.

Why Massachusetts Needs a Republican in Congress

The House of Representatives is the great hall of the people and is the branch of Congress that is closest to the people. As such it is not uncommon for citizen legislators like myself to be elected. One is less likely to find a career politician like Barney Frank in the House and more likely to find people like myself, people who have worked in the private sector and graduated from the school of hard knocks.

Frank's no vote on Amber Alert is a symptom of a congressman who has been in power too long and has grown accustomed to doing whatever he pleases. Twenty-five years, or twelve terms, of power and privilege have gone to Frank's head. Our district certainly deserves better.

As a Republican, I will be in a position to do more for the 4th district than my opponent. He has in fact admitted the impotency of the Democrats in the House, when he told a reporter, quoted in the *Washington Post* (11-25-03): "The Republican Party in the House is the most ideologically cohesive and disciplined in the democratic world." An astute observation by a very partisan politician. And there is great likelihood that Republicans will pick up even more seats in the next election.

Our President is a Republican, and I'm wagering that he will be re-elected to serve another four years. Both houses of Congress already have Republican majorities, and will most likely retain them, which means that Republicans will be in control of the debates and flow of legislation. A Republican from Massachusetts will find himself on the inside track of legislative events instead of on the outside like Frank.

Barney Frank: A Fourth District Liability

Yet Massachusetts still sends an all-Democratic delegation to Congress where they languish in the minority and are removed from positions of power and influence. I contend that Frank has become a liability to the district and is probably viewed as such by many Democrats as well.

To whom does Barney Frank turn when he wants something done for his district? President Bush, whom he has castigated? Dennis Hastert, Republic Speaker of the House? Tom DeLay, the Majority Leader who controls the legislative agenda? Or any of the Republican chairmen of House committees? Frank complains that he can't get approval for the New Bedford-Fall River commuter rail, an issue that he has done nothing to address in a quarter-century in Washington. Why should the House, or for that matter the Republican Governor of Massachusetts, be expected to now approve the financing of a project that would help an ultra-liberal get re-elected?

The New Bedford-Fall River Commuter Rail Line

As a Republican in Congress, I will be in an excellent position to get the much-needed New Bedford-Fall River Commuter Rail approved and financed. This is a transportation project the South Coast desperately needs. It will not only increase jobs but also provide businesses with better transit facilities for their employees and customers.

As a Republican, I will have the ear of the President, the Congressional leadership, and the Governor in advocating the building of that crucial addition to the South Coast's infrastructure. While in the past the powerful Boston Democrats in Washington were able to get a Democratic Congress to finance the Big Dig, those days are over. Only a Republican advocate from the 4th district will be able to find a sympathetic ear in Congress for the needs of the South Coast, long neglected by the Democrats.

The 4th congressional district needs to elect a Republican as the surest means of getting back into the mainstream of political power. Our district, particularly the South Coast, has been selling itself short for too long. We need a congressman who is focused on the business of the people of the 4th district and not on some national lifestyle agenda we have nothing to do with. We need a congressman who will be able to deliver what the district needs.

Frank's Response to the Media on Amber Alert

As a father of a young child, I was angry to learn that Frank had voted no on Amber Alert, and the many people I meet as I cross the district express shock and dismay as well. Frank's no vote on Amber Alert originally came to my attention due to a letter to the editor published in the *Mansfield News* and written by local Mansfield activist Lou Bertone who has since become a major supporter of my candidacy.

In response to this inexplicable vote I sent out a press release requesting the media to ask Frank why he voted no on Amber Alert. WBSM talk-show host Barry Richard responded by inviting me on his program in New Bedford to discuss the issue. The news department at WBSM also did a segment with me on the topic and called Frank in Washington to ask him to respond. Frank's response to Jack Peterson, a WBSM reporter, was that he had voted against Amber Alert because of "Republican add-ons." Frank had no problem with "add-ons" per se, in spite of his protestations, as he has a long record of voting for bills with all manner of pork-barrel, budget-busting add-ons. The astonishing response struck me as typical of Frank who has a reputation as an extreme partisan.

Amber Alert Was Nonpartisan,
But Barney Wasn't

Yet the Amber Alert legislation, known as the PROTECT Act, was clearly not a partisan bill since the entire Massachusetts congressional delegation, made up of all Democrats, had voted yes, all, except for Barney Frank. As the controversy mounted, Frank would essentially accuse his fellow Massachusetts Democratic congressmen, in an editorial in the *New Bedford Standard Times* entitled "Congressman supports the Amber Alert system" (8/29), of cowardice for voting yes on Amber Alert. Frank stated in the *Standard Times* editorial that his fellow Massachusetts Democrats voted yes under the duress of "legislative blackmail" in order to avoid the possibility of a "demagogic attack" from "right-wing" critics.

It certainly is news to me that opposition to Amber Alert and the other child protection measures included in the PROTECT Act is a "left-wing" cause since I would assume that "left-wingers" care as much about the safety of children as anyone else. Conversely, by implying that the yes vote on Amber Alert by the Massachusetts Democratic delegation was cowardly, it might be surmised that Frank views his no vote on the child protection measure to be a great act of virtue.

Barney Complains About the Republican Add-ons

After sending out another press release challenging Frank to identify which "Republican add-ons" in the PROTECT Act would cause him to vote against a bill that protects children from kidnappers, *Boston Globe* staff reporter Jonathan Saltzman interviewed both Frank and myself on the Amber Alert question. One of the questions Saltzman, a tough and professional reporter, asked me in the course of interviewing me was whether or not I viewed Frank's no vote on Amber Alert as having anything to do with his homosexual orientation. My response was an emphatic no followed by the assertion that I assumed that the gay community cared as much about the safety of children as I do, especially those who are themselves parents or guardians of minor children. I told Saltzman that I was convinced that most members of the gay community would join with me in supporting the child protection measure.

Frank's response to Saltzman, published in a *Boston Globe* article entitled "Critic of Rep. Frank mulls run in 2004" (8/28), was most revealing. In the article, Frank singled out two "Republican add-ons" that had caused him to vote no on Amber Alert. The first is known as the "two strikes you're out" law which calls for a mandatory minimum prison term for second time convicted child molesters. The second is the Rave Act, which makes it easier for federal prosecutors to close down venues where a promoter is knowingly and specifically promoting an event held for the purpose of allowing patrons to use illegal drugs such as ecstasy.

The only possible conclusion I can draw from Frank's response in the *Boston Globe* article is that he places the interests of cons and drug pushers over children. I regard the package of bills that includes Amber Alert to be a "bill of rights" for children. Every measure in the bill deals with protecting children and young people from criminals.

Other highlights of the PROTECT act include an expansion of wiretapping authority for the investigation of criminal sex cases involving children, a federal crime against the use of misleading internet domain names to lure people to pornography sites or to cause children to see "material that is harmful to minors," and a toughening of laws against sex tour operators. I am unable to find anything in the bill, anything whatsoever, that I don't wholeheartedly support. Neither, apparently did the rest of the all Democratic Massachusetts delegation including Senators Ted Kennedy and John Kerry.

Around the time of the *Boston Globe* article, Frank went on Barry Richard's WBSM radio show in New Bedford where he insisted that he actually did vote for Amber Alert in committee and that I was a demagogue for bringing this up. The fact of the matter is that when it really mattered, when the bill was on the floor for a full vote in Congress, a vote that would have made Amber Alert law, Frank voted no.

Barney Frank's Double Talk

Frank's assertion that he voted for the bill because he voted for aspects of it in committee is a classic example of a politician attempting to duck responsibility for his actions. Using these criteria, any politician could claim to have voted in favor of or against anything whatsoever if they side with either side of any issue in the process of making law. This type of hair splitting and double talk is typical of Frank.

I should mention that I happened to be listening to the radio when Richard interviewed Frank, an interview that was live and in person in the studio at WBSM, and I have rarely heard a more courageous and bare-knuckled interview than the one that Barry Richard conducted that day. After the interview, Richard told an associate of mine that when he brought up the issue of Amber Alert to the Congressman, Frank was literally trembling. Richard said that he had interviewed Frank over the years and that he had never seen him act in a manner other than as a tough and arrogant guy until that moment.

Richard also asked Frank why he was one of only seven congressmen out of 435 to vote no on a nonbinding resolution that expressed support for the Pledge of Allegiance to the Flag. This show of support by Congress followed the 9th Circuit Court of Appeals decision to strike "under God" from the pledge. Coincidentally, or perhaps not so coincidentally, shortly after the interview with Frank, Barry Richard, a longtime veteran of talk radio, and also a husband and father, was fired.

The Amber Alert vote is by no means the only vote cast by Frank that I will be examining in this campaign. I believe that this vote represents a symptom of a congressman who has been in power for too long and who has grown accustomed to doing whatever he wants with impunity. Twenty-five years of power and privilege have obviously gone to Frank's head and I believe that our district, our state, and our nation deserve better.

The Trend Toward Centralized Bureaucratic Government

A congressman does more than just simply bring home the bacon and provide constituent services as important as those functions are. We also ought to ask ourselves whether or not our congressman is acting in the best interest of the country. A congressman is in a position to shape the future of the nation and to set cultural trends. I believe in the ability and responsibility of the individual to determine his own destiny. There has been in recent decades a trend toward the transfer of those rights from the sovereign citizen, as expressed through their elected representatives, to an increasingly powerful and centralized bureaucratic government in Washington.

The gradual transfer of legislative responsibilities from elected officials to appointed bureaucrats and judges is a trend that troubles me. Congress ought to exercise its constitutional prerogative to override bureaucratic and judicial decrees. Bureaucracies ought to reflect and enforce the laws voted into existence by legislatures and the Judiciary ought to stick to it's constitutional mandate to review laws enacted by legislatures and to ensure that those laws stand up to constitutional muster.

The spectacle of judges and bureaucrats making law, a spectacle that is becoming more commonplace, is undemocratic and represents a trend toward a more authoritarian form of government than Americans have come to expect. If federal and state legislators, don't stand up to appointed officials, then eventually the chickens will come home to roost for all of us.

My View of Government

State government, with the Federal government playing a lesser role, ought to deal with the great moral questions of the day such as abortion regulation and the definition of marriage. State legislatures rather than judges and bureaucrats have traditionally decided such issues, which is the democratic approach and which is what has set this nation apart from more authoritarian nations.

I trust in the intrinsic wisdom of the American people as it is expressed through their elected officials who are charged to look to the constitution as their guide.

Government ought to provide a safety net, particularly for children, those with physical and mental handicaps, the elderly, and the infirm, but this does not mean that the government itself should run the programs. I support the granting of Federal funds to worthy charities and social agencies. President Bush has taken significant steps in this direction with his faith-based initiative, an initiative that Barney Frank opposes.

On Nightline with Ted Koppel, Frank expressed the preposterous view that the faith-based initiative was a sinister attempt, no doubt he sees it as right-wing, to coerce people into religion. Frank, who had previously voted against the Clinton welfare reform legislation, has a long record of supporting direct government control over social programs, an approach with a long record of failure.

I'm running for Congress because I want to help my friends and neighbors, my district, my state, and my country. We need to bring this district into the new economy of the 21st century by lowering taxes, eliminating unnecessary business regulation, reining in the bureaucracy, and improving the infrastructure.

We need to fight the war against the international terrorists who are conspiring to kill us and who already have. We need to protect children from predators who seek to harm them. We need to help America preserve its sovereignty by furthering the interests of the sovereign individual who derives his rights from the Creator. The Declaration of Independence tells us that the purpose of government is to protect and secure the God-given rights of the people, not to abrogate them. I seek a chance to serve in Congress with the hope that I can make a positive contribution to maintaining this precious heritage of freedom for our children.

How I became a Conservative

The best way for me to tackle the question of how I became a conservative is to start with my own story. How did I, Chuck Morse, a previously run-of-the-mill liberal, born and raised in a liberal atmosphere, become a conservative?

I trace my political transformation to a single date, April 7, 1986. That was the day I filled out my first tax return as a self-employed businessman. I had gone to "The Taxman" in Central Square, Cambridge, to get help in filling out the forms. At the time, I was filled with enthusiasm and idealism over the idea of filing my first return. It had been a promising first year in business and I was prepared to do my patriotic duty and pay my fair share.

When the accountant tabulated the initial figure in terms of what I would have to pay, it seemed like a lot of money but not an overwhelming amount. But then she informed me that she was not yet finished, she still had to tabulate my social security, Fica, State Tax, penalties for late payment, and other factors. My reaction to the final figure was total shock. I was dumbfounded. How was I going to come up with this much money? I would have to take the modest amount of money that I had accumulated in the course of the year, money that I had hoped to invest in expanding the business, and send it all to the government and then some. I was literally speechless.

The Turning Point

This proved to be a turning point for me. What exactly was the government doing with all this money? I had always believed that the government should provide social programs, but was the government actually helping people or merely fattening its own coffers? Was it really wise for government to take that much money out of a business, money that could have been used to increase production, creativity and jobs? Was the government helping or hurting working people, and did a safety net for the needy really have to come at such a high price? Couldn't it be done in a better way? And, besides, whose money was it anyway? These were some of the questions I started asking, and I began my own investigation.

What I discovered was that the old maxim, "Government that governs best governs least," was true. While I believe that government ought to play a role in providing a safety net for people, genuine social services do better when they're privately funded or when government provides assistance without actually getting into the business itself. I also discovered that, when left to their own devises, people are by and large very charitable and that most people want to do well and help their neighbor. I observed that when the government gets involved in running things, a level of social coercion kicks in and this is often counterproductive and leads to a negative outcome.

For example, in 1965, the Congress passed the Elementary and Secondary Education Act to help improve the public schools. Title One of the law provided compensatory education for minority children in the inner cities in order to help them learn to read and do math. After 39 years and untold billions of dollars, the gap between minority and white children in academics is as wide today as it was when the law was enacted. The problem is that those in charge of implementing Title One don't want it to succeed, because that would stop the flow of billions of dollars to the Title One establishment, those 50,000 directors, assistant directors, teachers, tutors, and specialists who live off the program.

The Spiritual Factor

The second aspect of my political transformation was more spiritual and occurred more gradually over time, and that involved my discovery of Judaism. I had grown up with a secular state of mind and was quite ignorant when it came to questions of the Jewish faith. My faith was summed up in the three basic tenets of secular Judaism: support for Israel, revulsion over the Nazi Holocaust, and a fear of anti-Semitism. While these basic tenets remain important to me, standing alone they nevertheless failed to provide a spiritual context that would guide my life and values.

My experience with the taxing arm of government had led me to believe that individuals did not have to depend on the State for services. So where, then, did the individual look for guidance if not the State? I'd always assumed that government was an instrument that could change man if controlled by enlightened people, but I now found that I could no longer accept this.

I found the answer in the Declaration of Independence, which declares, "We hold these truths to be self-evident, that all men are created equal, that they are endowed by their Creator with certain unalienable Rights, that among these are Life, Liberty and the pursuit of Happiness."

The Creator as the Source of Rights

I believe that the simple expression of faith contained in this line of the Declaration of Independence is completely in accord with Judaism, which is to say that we are endowed by "the Creator" or by the Lord God King of the Universe, a phrase that I am familiar with from Jewish prayer, with "certain unalienable rights" as opposed to being endowed by a State. The founders of this great Republic acknowledged as "self evident" that individual rights come from the Creator, as opposed to coming from the State, and this simple identification of the source of rights was and remains the most revolutionary and liberating idea known to man.

I believe that the simple acknowledgment of non-denominational faith contained in the Declaration has, more than any other factor, set this nation on a course that has led to the freest, most creative, most genuinely progressive, and most prosperous civilization in human history. America is a light unto the nations because Americans have understood that as individuals we are not beholden to the State.

The founding generation of Americans understood that human beings couldn't take the place of the Creator and declare the State as supreme because man is created in the image of the Creator and is therefore fallible. Only the Creator is perfect. Human beings are not.

When mankind attempts to create a perfect world by force, in violation of nature and nature's God, as Nimrod did with the Tower of Babel, and as both the Nazis and Communists attempted to do in modern times, the result is always ruinous and tragic.

When Men Worship the State

So then, why have so many Americans been seduced by the siren song of big government liberalism? By this I mean why have so many Americans been attracted to a form of worship of the State as opposed to a simple worship of God or acceptance of common reason? Why have so many Americans viewed government as a messianic force as opposed to their own understanding of self-determination under God and individual salvation? Why have so many Americans fallen for the false god of collectivism as opposed to the idea of personal responsibility and redemption? Why have so many Americans, in this day and age, embraced the regressive idea of worshiping state power as opposed to the self-evident understanding that rights and responsibilities come from the Creator?

On July 4, 1776, the American colonists declared their independence from the autocratic tyranny of King George III of England. The issue that finally brought things to a boil, even though most of the colonists would have preferred to find a means of remaining loyal British subjects, was the increasingly bare and open display of total fiat power being demonstrated by the British tyrant.

The American colonists had enjoyed self-government and much freedom in the early days of settlement, and now they saw those freedoms being whittled away by a tyrannical king. And so they decided to fight back, because they cherished freedom and knew they were capable of self-rule and controlling their own destiny. After driving the British out at considerable sacrifice in blood and treasure, the founding generation was careful not to replicate the foreign autocracy with a homegrown version when they crafted the Constitution of 1788.

A respect for individual rights and property rights led to an economic expansion that remains unparalleled in history. Set on the road toward an enlightened view of rights, America abolished the barbarous institution of chattel slavery after a bloody civil war and moved toward full citizenship rights for women. The American idea of progress, which is also the conservative idea of progress, was and remains the advancement of greater rights for the individual.

The Road Back to Serfdom

Yet starting in the early 20th century, many Americans embraced the neo-monarchical principles of socialism, which constituted a regressive return to the old world idea of the divine right of Kings. Modern socialism replaced the King with an elite cadre of "enlightened" intellectuals and the new divine right of "science."

Some Americans even embraced the totalitarian faith of Communism, a faith that considers the State to be all-powerful and recognizes no inherent rights whatsoever for the individual. Communism attempted to replace God with the promise that the State would bring about human redemption and utopia at the hand of an enlightened and properly educated elite. The phenomenon of any American, lucky enough to be born and/or live in the land of milk and honey, embracing such a system of total human bondage, is a strange one indeed.

Yet the lure of Communism was the idea that human nature could be changed by force with the State serving as the blunt instrument of change. Conservatism asserts the exact opposite principle, which is that the individual is capable of change and that the change must be inspired by such notions as free will, faith, incentive, and self-interest. America is essentially a conservative society because we honor the idea of individual self-interest.

America remains the greatest experiment in self-rule the world has ever known. The sovereign individual, endowed by the Creator with certain unalienable rights, is an idea that is at the core of American conservatism and continues to find expression throughout America and rarely elsewhere. Yet the regressive encroachment of big, socialistic, hyper-nationalistic government is costing us dearly, and the cost is lost freedom and increased subservience to government. Freedom doesn't grow on trees. Our forefathers fought for freedom and every generation must grapple with threats to freedom. This generation is no different, and my hope and prayer is that this generation is able and willing to live up to the challenge.

Am I "right-wing?"

As predictable as the rising sun, my opponent, Congressman Barney Frank, is calling me "right wing" in the media. Frank has a long and nasty history of attacking virtually anyone who dares to disagree with him with names such as right wing, racist, bigot, extremist, etc. I believe that the citizens of the 4th Congressional District are wise enough to see through this type of character assassination and understand that Frank has drawn from this poisonous well too many times to be credible. Frank has been known to see a right-winger hiding under every bed and lurking behind every corner.

I hope people see this for what it is: an attempt by Frank to avoid a genuine dialogue on the issues by attempting to strangle his opponent in the crib. This district hasn't had a real campaign for Congress in almost a quarter of a century. Let's not allow Barney Frank to deny us the opportunity to have a real debate, a debate that will greatly benefit the voters of the district. Let's not throw this opportunity away by allowing Frank to engage in a campaign of smear and denunciation.

Frank recently called me "a very right wing guy" on a radio station in the Fall River area. When I listened to him make the charge, and heard the shrill tone of his remarks following the charge, I was brought back to my third-grade schoolyard in Quincy where a bully had once taunted me with the charge that I was a dirty Jew. I hid inside the school during recess for a couple of days. After a while I got sick of hiding and my fear was replaced by anger and defiance. I decided to stride forth into the schoolyard and let the chips fall where they may. If the bully wanted a fight then so be it. When the bully saw me in the schoolyard and saw that I wasn't going to be intimidated, he dropped his bullyboy stance and the episode was over.

One of my books is facetiously entitled "Why I'm a Right-Wing Extremist." The title was meant to be politically satiric, mainly to get public attention. Using such a provocative title was the equivalent of calling the book "Why I'm a Son of a Bitch." Nevertheless, by giving the book this title I left myself wide open for the type of scurrilous attack that was inevitable anyway. I owe the public an explanation, however, regarding what I meant by calling myself a "right-wing extremist."

What Happens When You
Oppose Political Correctness

I'm a right-wing extremist because people like Barney Frank say that I am. Anyone who takes a position that is not deemed to be politically correct, as the term is defined by liberal cultural elites, runs the risk of being denounced as right wing, an extremist, or whatever slur is in vogue. Political correctness is, of course, an arbitrary designation and what might be considered politically correct at one point may not be so at another point in time.

I would contend that the term "right-wing" in America today, unless we're talking about neo-Nazis or some other extreme fringe group, is generally one that can be applied to anyone who runs afoul of politically correct positions of the left.

Historically, a person or group might be called right wing if that person or group dissented from the party line of the Communist Party. For example, in the 1930's, Leon Trotsky and his American followers were called right wing by the followers of Stalin because the Trotskyites were not as far to the left as the Stalinists. The fact that Trotsky was a bona fide Communist himself, one of the principle participants in the 1917 Bolshevik coup in Russia, and the founder of the Soviet Red Army, was irrelevant. Moderates, liberals, and even leftists run the risk of being denounced as right wing if they stick their necks out too far and take a definitive stand against what passes as politically correct.

The Pressure to Conform

Understandably, most people would rather keep their heads low and conform than subject themselves to the abuse that might accompany the taking of a clear stand against a politically correct position. The atmosphere of political correctness in this county is becoming increasingly stultifying and oppressive.

I would make the case that at the present time, the term "right-wing" has little if anything to do with the actual political convictions of the person being subjected to the charge and that this is certainly true in my case. Well than, why do so many well meaning people who have no discernable ulterior motive draw the conclusion that I am "right wing" after hearing me speak or after reading one of my columns?

In order to present a theory to answer this question, a bit of background is in order. I am a Jew. Family members on my mother's side were killed in the Nazi Holocaust against the Jews. As a child I heard a great deal of discussion about the Holocaust at the dinner table, especially when the extended family got together. As a result, I developed an interest in the Holocaust, the nature of Nazism, and how it all came to be. When I was in the sixth grade I read *The Rise and Fall of the Third Reich* by William Shirer, the correspondent for Time magazine in Nazi Germany in the 1930's. Shirer's book remains a definitive and widely respected history of Nazi Germany and I remember reading it carefully and being greatly affected by it.

Communism and Nazism Are the Same

As I delved more deeply over the years into a serious study of the nature of Nazism as a political and social phenomenon, as a means of gaining insight into the cause of the Holocaust and how such evil could be prevented, I began simultaneously to study the nature of Communism. I began to compare and contrast the two political, economic, social, and spiritual systems, and I eventually concluded that there wasn't a dime's worth of difference between the two.

There is no single event in history more evil or monstrous than the Nazi Holocaust against the Jews. It should be noted, however, that international Communism was responsible for the murder of four times as many human beings as were killed by Nazis.

I came to realize that both political movements required the total surrender of the freedoms of its citizens under the guise that such a sacrifice was in the best interest of the people and the future. Both movements were animated by the utopian idea that human nature can be perfected by force, and both movements sought to liquidate those who were perceived as standing in the way. While the Nazis believed that the Jews were the primary obstacles to their creation of the ubermench, or Master Race, the Communists believed the obstacle was the middle-class property-owner, referred to in Communist literature as the Bourgeoisie, all of whom, along with believers in God, were deemed to be politically incorrect.

If those who embraced a Nazi philosophy came to play a dominant role in America, then I would hope that I would have the courage to criticize Nazism. The reason I've written so critically about Communism and its sphere of influence in this country is because, for whatever reason, Communism, instead of Nazism, has wielded a profound influence on our philosophy and thinking, especially in our universities.

I'm not suggesting that the American left, which euphemistically calls itself "progressive," is a Nazi like movement, nor am I comparing American leftists to Nazis per se. I also understand the anger and rage that so many so-called "progressives" have expressed toward me when confronted with my ideas, as I too would not want to think that anyone was comparing me to a Nazi either.

The Unprogressive Progressives

The truth of the matter is that most of the so-called "progressives" in this country are completely unwitting regarding the true nature and underpinnings of the political faith they've embraced. As I see it, most American "progressives" get involved out of a craving for social acceptance, as most people naturally want to be counted as one of the beautiful people.

There is also a subtle and unspoken threat that if one doesn't genuflect, at least slightly, toward the "progressives," then one will pay the price in social ostracism and perhaps a loss of position in the community. Social pressure is a powerful force as a lack of acceptance could adversely affect one's family and one's income level. These are not minor considerations. In educational circles such social pressure is often referred to as a form of Group Dynamics.

Perhaps a subtle and informal conditioning sets in, usually at an early age, which leads many to stop questioning issues too deeply and to accept the politically correct view as the road of least resistance. Additionally, every so often a person who fails to conform is publicly disemboweled as an example to others of what might happen if one strays too far off the politically correct plantation. History is, of course, replete with extreme and overt examples of this, and one that comes to my mind is the Spanish Inquisition.

So people think that I sound right wing simply because I've been an outspoken critic of communism and its influence on our society, and most people aren't used to hearing such criticism. The designation actually has nothing to do with my views *per se,* and I've noticed that most of those who have made this accusation against me know nothing about my views and aren't interested in knowing. The charge is based on a fear of someone who might be different, and the attitude behind the charge often borders on outright bigotry.

The hallmark of the Nazi and Communist faiths is that human nature can be changed and perfected by force. A conservative recognizes the fallen nature of man, that man cannot be perfected. Since man will never completely eradicate the darker side of his nature, such as crime, racism, or intolerance, the best course of action, advocated by conservatives, is to make the necessary improvements in our society while preserving individual liberty.

The Great Controversy Over Gay Marriage

The question of gay marriage has hit the political and social landscape of America like a thunderclap. For starters, the gay community should be encouraged to form monogamous unions if, for no other reason, than to reduce the promiscuous sexual behavior that encourages the spread of AIDS and other diseases. The definition of marriage however, should, in my view, remain exclusively the prerogative of the heterosexual couple.

My position on gay marriage, a position that is also held by all of the major Democratic candidates for the Presidency, is not discriminatory against gay people. It is not discriminatory because the present definition of marriage is between one man and one woman who must both be of legal age, neither of whom can be married to another at the time of the marriage, and neither of whom can be a close blood relative. Marriage excludes all categories that don't meet these criteria, so marriage as it is presently defined is not discriminatory against any one group.

By the way, a recent survey of public attitudes toward gay marriage reports that the vast majority of Americans oppose it. The survey also found that Americans who support gay marriage tend to be young, single, childless, liberal, oriented toward the Democratic Party, and not intensely involved in organized religion. An article in the *New York Times* that appeared shortly after the Massachusetts SJC ruling on gay marriage, indicated that the vast majority of gays interviewed by the *Times* had no interest in obtaining marriage licenses themselves.

Why Base Civil Unions Only on Sex?

So what about the idea of civil unions for gays that, as far as I can tell, are an arrangement that would give gay couples most of the privileges afforded hetero-sexual couples without the formal title? It seems to me that if such unions were to become legally recognized, they should be based on number of dependants rather than on whether or not there is a sexual relationship. For example, I have a friend who works for the City of Cambridge. He lives with and cares for two elderly aunts, both of whom are in their mid-to-late eighties and who are in varying degrees of declining health. Why shouldn't he and his two aunts qualify for civil union benefits?

What if, as in another case, two or more men who are not gay live together and are caring for a minor child, or an elderly parent, or a sick veteran, or some-one who is physically or mentally handicapped. Why shouldn't they qualify for civil union benefits? If civil unions are to be recognized as legal entities, it seems to me that the criteria for such unions should be based on number of dependants rather than on a sexual relationship.

The Nucleus of the Nuclear Family

So, should civil unions, or any form of alternative family, achieve legal recognition? This is a complex question worthy of debate over a long period of time. Marriage between one man and one woman, the nucleus of the nuclear family, has been a recognized institution since the days of the Romans and before. The first married couple, according to the Bible, was Adam and Eve.

While polygamy has existed to varying degrees in many cultures, nevertheless the model of the single couple has been generally held up as a universal ideal by most societies, with steps taken to foster its development. I remember reading a novel by Pearl S.Buck, *The Good Earth,* in which it was clear that in 19th century China, while some men had more than one wife, the practice was frowned upon and was rife with problems. Large portions of the Bible deal with all of the complex problems the Patriarchs dealt with as a result of having more than one wife.

Societies have historically been willing to make certain concessions in order to encourage marriage, and America is no exception. The married man has traditionally been given preference in the job market mainly because of dependant children, and the married working woman with children has also received special consideration in the workplace.

Unmarried people, perhaps grudgingly at times, have been willing to accord special privileges to married couples in the interest of furthering the family, which forms the strong basis of our social fabric. Businesses have also been asked to make concessions to married employees by assuming certain out-of-pocket expenses as well as the occasional slowdown in production.

The Cost of Special Privileges

The salient question is whether or not society and the business community are willing to expand the special privileges traditionally granted to the married couple to a broader population seeking marriage benefits. Is such an expansion a good idea economically? Already enhanced benefits granted by businesses to employees have driven up the cost of production, the cost of goods and services to the consumer, and have caused a contraction in industry with jobs going overseas. These are considerations that need to be taken very seriously before rushing into an expansion of marriage benefits under the law.

Since my opponent, Congressman Barney Frank is a leading advocate for gay rights and is a self-described gay leader, it is appropriate for me to comment on this issue. I should note that if my opponent were Congressmen Bill Delahunt or James McGovern this wouldn't likely be necessary.

Are All Opponents of Gay Marriage Homophobes?

Frank has a history of calling anyone who opposes the gay agenda a homophobe or a bigot as he did recently in an article posted on his website dealing with the Supreme Court Lawrence decision, which struck down the Texas sodomy laws. While I agree with the Lawrence decision, I disagree with Frank's intemperate description in his article of Justice Antonin Scalia, calling him a "bigot" for writing the opposing opinion. He also called Pennsylvania Senator Rick Santorum a "bigot" for his opposition to the decision.

In the same article, Frank compared a previous Supreme Court decision, which upheld sodomy laws, the Hardwick decision, to the Dred Scott decision, which upheld chattel slavery in 1859. The comparison between a Supreme Court decision that, however wrongly, upholds a state law that bans homosexual sex to a Supreme Court decision that upheld the institution of slavery for people who were brought to this continent in chains, really borders on the bizarre. I wouldn't blame African Americans if they were offended, as I am, by such a contorted comparison. Since Frank compares Hardwick to Dred Scott, perhaps he conversely compares Lawrence to the Emancipation Proclamation.

When Republican Brookline Attorney Jonathan Raymond ran against Frank for Congress in 1996, rumors surfaced in the last week of the campaign that Raymond was a homophobe, and I certainly expect the same type of dirty and despicable tactic to be used against me. Perhaps the gay community should actually consider supporting me rather than Frank because, for the most part, I want the same things that they most likely want.

Like myself, most gays I believe are tired of having to pay over 40% if their annual income in taxes and are tired of business regulations that impede business. Like myself, most gays are as concerned about terrorism as I am, and want a vigorous and swift defeat of these criminals. After all, there were gays undoubtedly killed in the World Trade Center in New York. Like myself, most gays care about the safety of minors and support Amber Alert and the other child safety measures.

And, while I have no proof to back this up, I sense that many gays are growing more conservative.

Where Was Gay Leadership
When It Was Badly Needed?

I'd like to bring up a question that has bothered me for years. When the AIDS epidemic first came to light in the early 1980's, it was common knowledge, even back then, that one of the ways AIDS was spread was by means of certain sexual practices, particularly anal sex. I found out at a high-school reunion in the mid 1980's that a friend who had lived near me when I was growing up in Quincy had died of AIDS. Someone that I worked with around that same time also contracted AIDS and died a terrible death. I'm sure that most of the readers of this book know of someone who has died of AIDS.

Why then, with all that was known about how AIDS is spread, didn't a prominent figure in the gay community come out and warn gay men in particular about how AIDS is spread? Why didn't any prominent gay leader tell gay men to stop the practices that were spreading AIDS? Why didn't the gay community close down the bath houses, for example, which were incubators for the spread of this ghastly disease?

If AIDS had been treated as any other contagious and deadly disease, who knows, perhaps tens of thousands of innocent young men might be alive today. If gay men had heard even one prominent gay leader speak up and tell them to stop the behavior that was spreading AIDS, at least until the disease was under control, untold numbers might not have had to suffer the horrors of this miserable disease. Perhaps if a prominent gay leader, such as Congressman Barney Frank, who was serving in Congress during those years, had the courage to speak up, who knows how many men might have been spared the unspeakable suffering and death that AIDS causes.

National Security

Any sane sovereign nation, worthy of the term, takes proper steps to protect the lives and property of its citizens both domestically and abroad. America is the richest and most powerful nation on earth and, as such, extraordinary measures are appropriate in order to fulfill this obligation. As a result of their own putrid economic systems, their lack of liberty, lack of private property, a middle class, and democratic institutions, many nations of the world lag far behind us politically, economically and spiritually. As a result, many peoples of the world, unfortunate enough to live in these nations, cast an envious eye on our golden shores.

While we ought to encourage and assist foreign nations who seek to move toward freedom and help those who seek to adopt approaches that have worked so well for us, we must at the same time be ever vigilant in defending ourselves against those backward nations that remain in the iron grip of totalitarianism.

The leaders of many of these nations often attempt to shift attention away from their own failures by scapegoating America with the false claim that somehow American success has been achieved at their expense. These types of lies, often promoted by regimes that control their own media, can contribute to the development of individuals and groups who seek to kill Americans and destroy America. Perhaps they believe that by destroying America, somehow their own problems will be alleviated.

The Need for a Strong Defense

Because of our position in the world, we must maintain a military that is, besides equipped to defend the homeland, also able to engage in missions around the world if need be. America has a long tradition of liberating populations from oppression going back to the liberation of Cuba from Spain in 1898 and the liberation of most of Europe and the Pacific Rim from Nazism and Japanese Imperialism.

President Ronald Reagan picked up the standard when he accurately identified the Soviet Union as an evil empire and he backed up that rhetoric with actions that greatly contributed to the disintegration of Communist oppression in Russia and Eastern Europe.

Today, President George W. Bush carries on this great moral tradition by lending his firm and resolute leadership in the cause of liberating Iraq from the brutal clutches of Saddam Hussein and Baath Party socialism. America has been, is, and will, God willing, continue to be a moral force in the world as long as its citizens have the will to maintain a strong military and as long as brave American men and women are willing to serve in that military.

Barney Frank's Defeatism

My opponent, Congressman Barney Frank, embraces a different defeatist idea, one that claims that if America disarms, if America cuts back its military, then somehow, miraculously, the world will become more peaceful. Frank has consistently voted to cut the defense budget during his entire tenure in Congress.

Frank voted against the strategic defense initiative in the 1980's, an initiative which involved research into the possibility of developing a nuclear shield. Had that research borne fruit, a nuclear shield would have effectively rendered nuclear missiles obsolete, and there would be no nuclear threat from North Korea today.

Frank voted to hamstring the CIA in the 1990's by supporting a bill that prevented it from recruiting "unsavory characters" thus impeding its ability to investigate terrorism in the years leading up to the attack on the World Trade Center and Pentagon on September 11, 2001. In the aftermath of 9/11, Frank has tried to prevent the government from taking appropriate emergency measures to protect American lives from the terrorist conspiracy by opposing the USA Patriot Act. Most of the provisions of the Patriot Act are due to expire at the end of 2005, assuming the emergency is over by then. Such measures have been taken by American administrations during wartime going back to General George Washington who conducted military trials while fighting the American Revolution.

Frank Opposed the Homeland Security Act

Frank opposed appropriations to Homeland Security. Recently, Frank has picked up the standard of the terrorists being detained at Guantanamo Bay, this while we live under the threat of terrorists hijacking passenger planes in order to use them as missiles to kill as many Americans as possible.

Frank voted against both Iraq wars, and rarely does he speak on the floor of the House when, at some point, he doesn't make a sarcastic remark about military spending. This foolish approach used to constitute silly utopian fantasies, but since 9/11, most Americans now understand what most conservatives have always understood, which is that this type of anti-defense approach costs lives and endangers the peace.

Barney's Conspiracy Theory

Last August, according to the *Brookline Tab,* Barney Frank told a roomful of impressionable Brookline High School students that the President of the United States was a liar. He wove a sinister conspiracy theory of a government plot by, no doubt, a group of right-wingers, to drag America into an invasion of Iraq under the false pretence that the Iraqis were in the process of acquiring weapons of mass destruction.

This is a very serious charge to make against a sitting President, and I would like to see Frank deliver some proof of this. It's one thing for an author or a media figure to espouse a crackpot conspiracy theory, many of which I listened to on talk-radio, but when a sitting congressman sallies forth with such charges, and feels no need to provide documentation for his cockamamie theory, then you have a matter altogether different.

Given the fact that former President Bill Clinton, former Secretary of State Madeline Albright, most heads of state in the world, and most members of Congress, also believed that the Iraqis were attempting to develop weapons of mass destruction, it would be reasonable to ask Frank if all of them were in on this sinister plot he described to the impressionable students at Brookline High that day. And while we're at it, it would stand to reason to ask Frank to explain exactly what he thinks the motive would have been for the government to engage in such a plot.

The Present Crisis as a Political Football

This type of irresponsible speculation has a demoralizing effect at a time when the American military is struggling to accomplish a very difficult mission. Such talk emboldens the enemies of peace and thus may very well contribute to the deaths of Americans. This approach to the present crisis on the part of Frank, entirely driven by domestic partisan considerations, is jeopardizing the war against international terrorism and is probably putting all of us at serious risk. We need to get serious in this war against terrorism and stop using this crisis as a political football.

Frank is one of those who complain that American operations in Iraq are not under the auspices of the United Nations but should be. While I do not, nor have I ever advocated that America pull out of the United Nations, nevertheless, I believe that our sovereign Republic must primarily operate in the interests of the American people as it is construed by their elected representatives in Congress and in the White House.

While I support the principle of America working with like-minded allies around the world, as in Iraq, where President Bush has referred to our many allies in that effort as "the coalition of the willing," I nevertheless believe that such alliances should avoid permanent entanglements whenever possible.

While the United Nations certainly ought to play a humanitarian role in world affairs, that role ought to take a back seat to the rights of sovereign nations, as the United Nations has generally proven itself to be an amoral force in the world.

To preserve and protect the lives of Americans today, and those of future generations, America must maintain as strong a military position in the world as possible. To preserve and protect our democracy and our sovereign rights as citizens, America must at the same time avoid entangling alliances. Our government must be committed to placing American interests first and without apologies. To ensure a more peaceful world, America must reach out the hand of friendship and trade to like-minded nations while at the same time we must seek out and utterly smite those enemies of freedom who seek to kill us.

Conclusion

I hope that this short volume provides some insights into my views and why I am seeking the office of Representative from the 4th Congressional District of Massachusetts in 2004. Please know that I am more than happy to answer any questions you might have.

As I cross the district in the course of this campaign, I hope to have the opportunity to meet you and directly learn about your concerns. Running for office has, so far, been a wonderful experience, one that I wouldn't trade for anything. I am gaining great first-hand insights into how our political system works, what it means to be an American, and I'm grateful for the opportunity.

An election is a peaceful revolution. Every election cycle represents a form of warfare without violence, and the fact that this nation has seen elections uninterrupted by violence or coercion since 1789 is truly an awe-inspiring thing to contemplate.

An election should offer the voter a vivid and, at times, a heated exchange of conflicting ideas. A nice election where everyone holds hands and gets along and has only one candidate to vote for only happens in places like Communist Cuba or North Korea. But here at home, the voters will have the opportunity to choose which set of ideas most represents their own, and that choice will find its expression in the voting booth.

The 4th Congressional District hasn't had a real contest in almost a quarter of a century and a lot has changed in those years. I believe that I can play a role in bringing our district into the 21st century by introducing and hopefully enacting laws that support business growth and rescinding laws that impede that growth. The people of our district need tax relief, a fiscally responsible government that will not burden future generations with inflation and debt, and an improvement in infrastructure to help stimulate job creation and improve the quality of life.

The Republican Party is in the ascendance both in Massachusetts and in Washington, and I contend that our district would benefit greatly by sending an energetic, committed Republican to Congress. As a Republican, I believe that I'll be in the best position to get things done for our district.

Time has passed Barney Frank by, he's out of time and he's out of gas. It's time for a change. It's time for the 4th Congressional District and Massachusetts to enter the mainstream of 21st century politics. Please support my candidacy and, if you want to bring about real change for our district, vote for me on Tuesday, November 2, 2004.

A Note of Thanks

Ever since I embarked on this journey into the world of talk-radio and politics, I have had the good fortune of getting to know people who have encouraged me along the way. One such person is Sam Blumenfeld, writer of books on education and literacy, whom I first interviewed some seven years ago. He has since become a good friend and shared many a night as a co-host on my show. He encouraged me to write columns which have appeared on many internet websites and which were compiled in four books.

But the greatest encouragement has come from my wife, Barbara, who has given me the freedom to spread my wings. She and my daughter are what make life worth living and fighting for.

I also wish to thank all of those great people who have seen fit to help this campaign get started: Anthony Ciciariello, National Republican Committee-woman Jody Dow, Ambassador Margaret Heckler, Ben Kilgore, Chris McCarthy, and Phil Paleologos,

PERSONAL REPLY TO CHUCK MORSE

( ) **YES,** I believe it is time to beat Barney Frank.

Name_____email_____
Address_____phone_____
City/Town_____ Zip_____

To help your campaign, I am sending a contribution of

( ) $2000 ( ) $1000 ( ) $500 ( ) $250 ( ) $150 ( ) $100 ( ) $50
( ) Other_____

I will help Chuck by doing the following

( ) Putting a bumbersticker on my car ( ) volunteering
( ) Drop Literature ( ) Host a fundraiser
( ) Put a sign on my lawn

Federal law requires us to use our best efforts and report the name, address, occupation and name of employer for individuals whose contributions exceed $200 in a calendar year. The maximum contribution is $2000 per individual—$4000 per couple per election. Federal law prohibits corporate contributions. Political contributions are not tax deductible as charitable contributions for income tax purposes.

Mailing Address

Morse For Congress 2004
258 Harvard Street #240
Brookline, MA 02446

Phone Number   1-800-272-7324
For media inquiries, please call Ben Kilgore at: 1-978-448-8577

Please consider making an online contribution at
www.morseforcongress.com

PERSONAL REPLY TO CHUCK MORSE

( ) **YES,** I believe it is time to beat Barney Frank.

Name_____email_____
Address_____phone_____
City/Town_____ Zip_____

To help your campaign, I am sending a contribution of

( ) $2000 ( ) $1000 ( ) $500 ( ) $250 ( ) $150 ( ) $100 ( ) $50
( ) Other_____

I will help Chuck by doing the following

( ) Putting a bumbersticker on my car   ( ) volunteering
( ) Drop Literature   ( ) Host a fundraiser
( ) Put a sign on my lawn

Federal law requires us to use our best efforts and report the name, address, occupation and name of employer for individuals whose contributions exceed $200 in a calendar year. The maximum contribution is $2000 per individual—$4000 per couple per election. Federal law prohibits corporate contributions. Political contributions are not tax deductible as charitable contributions for income tax purposes.

Mailing Address

Morse For Congress 2004
258 Harvard Street #240
Brookline, MA 02446

Phone Number   1-800-272-7324
For media inquiries, please call Ben Kilgore at: 1-978-448-8577

Please consider making an online contribution at
www.morseforcongress.com

PERSONAL REPLY TO CHUCK MORSE

( ) **YES,** I believe it is time to beat Barney Frank.

Name_____email_____
Address_____phone_____
City/Town_____ Zip_____

To help your campaign, I am sending a contribution of

( ) $2000 ( ) $1000 ( ) $500 ( ) $250 ( ) $150 ( ) $100 ( ) $50
( ) Other_____

I will help Chuck by doing the following

( ) Putting a bumbersticker on my car   ( ) volunteering
( ) Drop Literature   ( ) Host a fundraiser
( ) Put a sign on my lawn

Federal law requires us to use our best efforts and report the name, address, occupation and name of employer for individuals whose contributions exceed $200 in a calendar year. The maximum contribution is $2000 per individual—$4000 per couple per election. Federal law prohibits corporate contributions. Political contributions are not tax deductible as charitable contributions for income tax purposes.

Mailing Address

Morse For Congress 2004
258 Harvard Street #240
Brookline, MA 02446

Phone Number   1-800-272-7324
For media inquiries, please call Ben Kilgore at: 1-978-448-8577

Please consider making an online contribution at
www.morseforcongress.com

0-595-30766-3